Extreme Ed's Air Adventures

Dee White
Illustrated by Nahum Ziersch

Contents

Skydiving

Ed loves **extreme** sports. One of his favourite sports to watch is skydiving.

Skydivers jump from a plane high in the air. They fall freely through the air, then they open their parachutes. They float safely to the ground.

Did You Know ?

Sometimes, skydivers use their parachutes to jump off towers, bridges and cliffs. This is called **base jumping**.

This skydiver is about to jump out of the plane. The side door of the plane is open. The skydiver sits on the edge with his legs dangling over the side. "Woohoo!" he shouts as he jumps.

His parachute opens and the skydiver floats to the ground like a leaf.

Ed goes to watch skydiving at a special skydiving centre. He watches the planes fly up into the sky. The skydivers jump out and land on the ground.

Some people skydive with another person. This is called **tandem** skydiving.

Wingsuit Flying

This man is a wingsuit flier. He is dressed in a special wingsuit. It has two wings for the arms and a tail for the legs.

Wingsuit fliers jump out of a plane or from a high place. They soar through the air like a bird. Then they open their parachute and land safely on the ground.

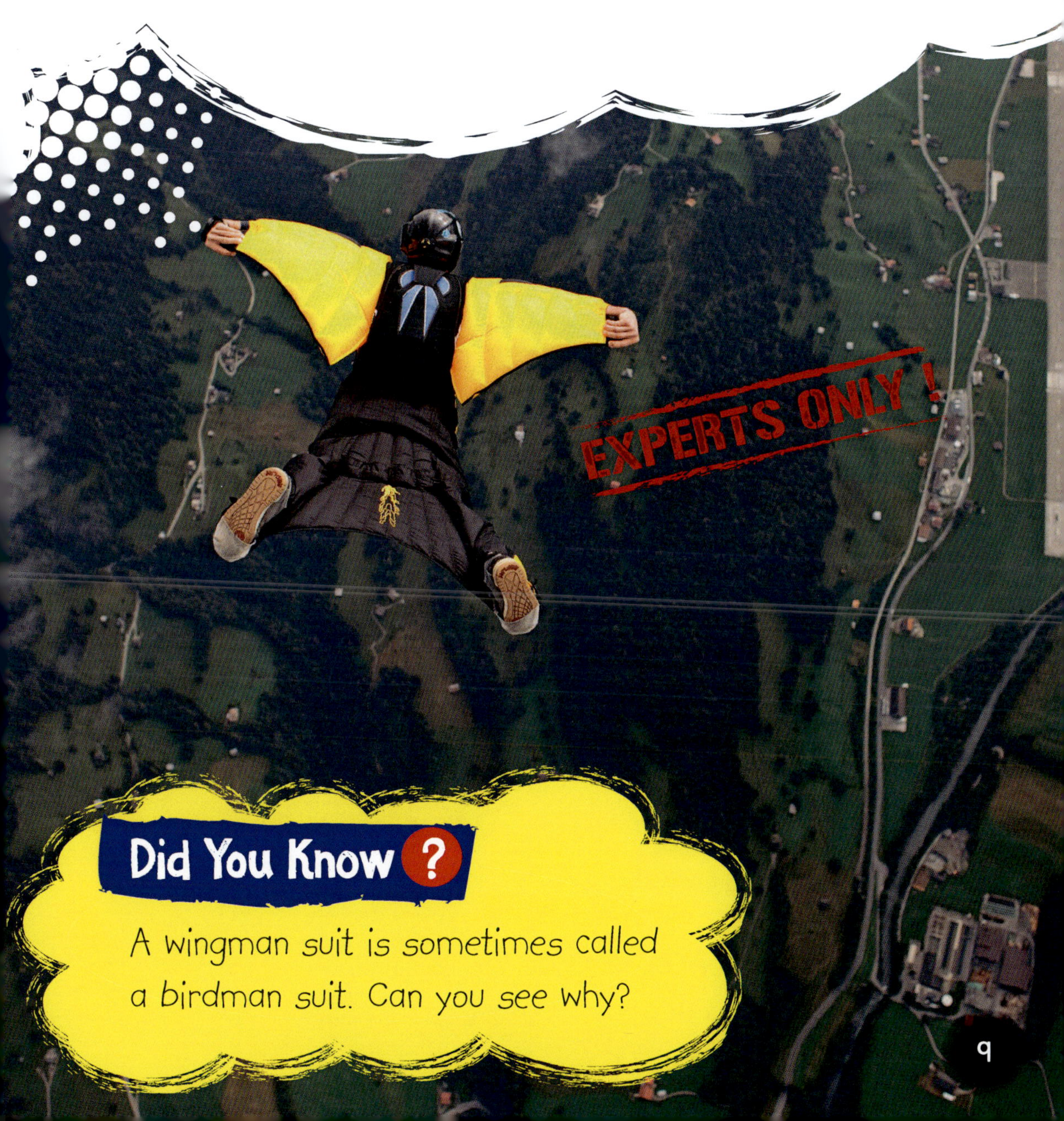

Did You Know?

A wingman suit is sometimes called a birdman suit. Can you see why?

Wingsuit flying can be dangerous. You have to get your hands out of the wings while you are in the air to open the parachute.

Look at this wingsuit flier! He has opened his parachute. He floats safely to the ground.

Tandem Skydiving

Ed likes to watch his friend Andy skydive. Andy is in a wheelchair, so he does tandem skydiving. He is strapped to another skydiver for their jump.

Did You Know?

Some people skydive strapped into their wheelchairs.

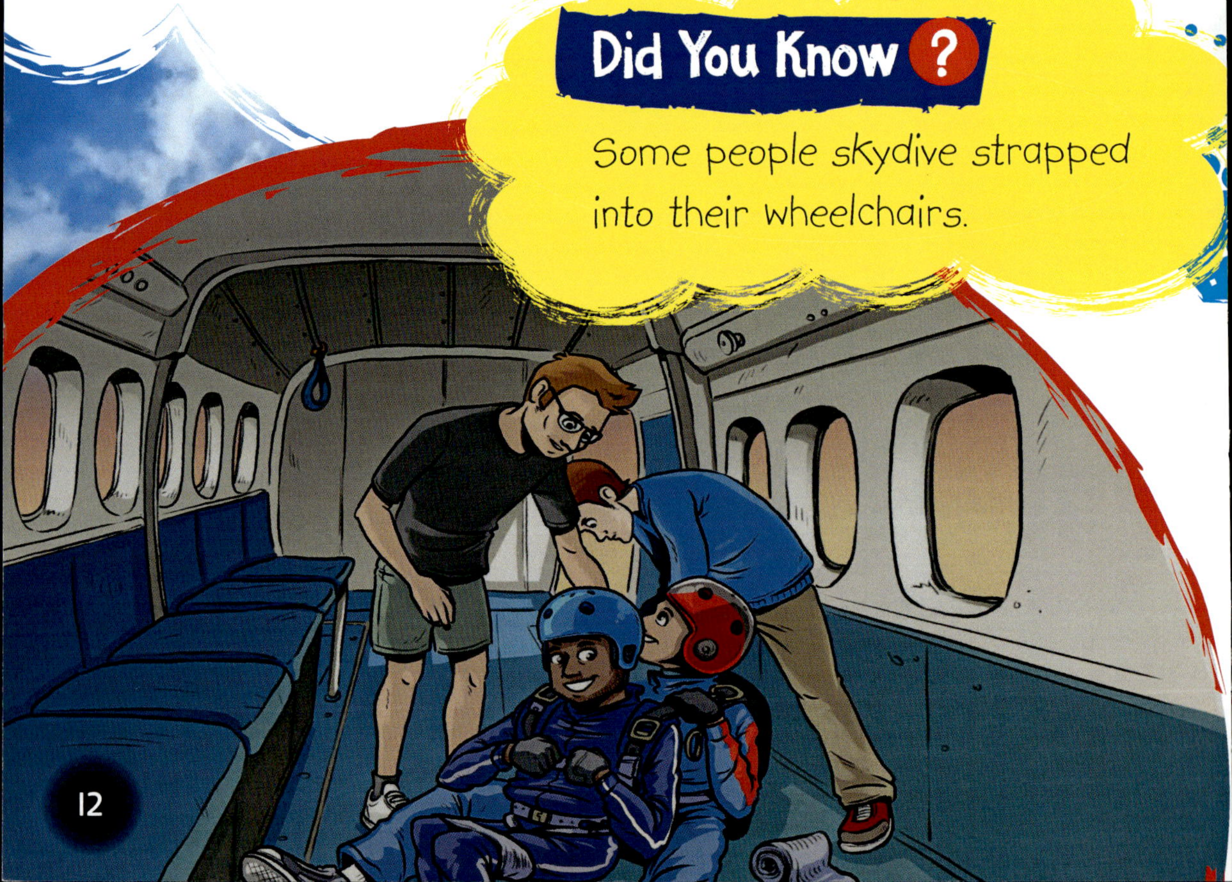

When it is time to jump, Andy's partner helps him to hang his legs over the edge of the plane.

Andy and his partner jump out of the plane.

They hold out their arms and fall through the air. Then Andy's partner opens the parachute. They float to the ground and land there safely.

Hang-Gliding

You can also fly through the air using a hang-glider. Ed wants to try hang-gliding when he grows up.

EXPERTS ONLY !

A hang-glider has a frame that is shaped like a wing. It has a cloth stretched over it. The hang-glider does not have a **motor**.

The pilot is put into a **harness**. They are connected to another frame that is shaped like a triangle.

This man helps the hang-glider take off from the ground.

The frame is like a steering wheel. The pilot moves the frame to turn the hang-glider.

Hot Air Ballooning

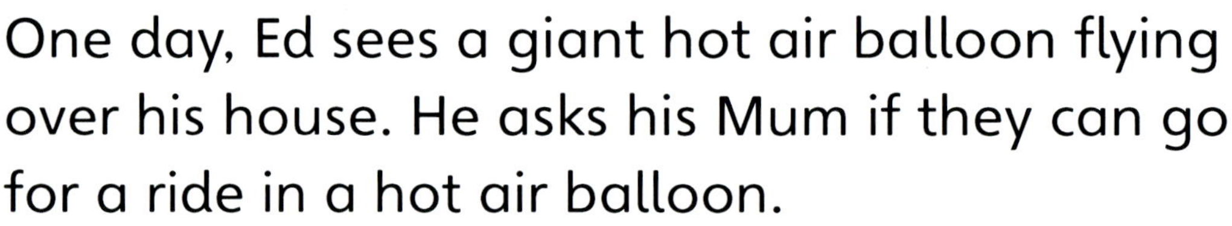

One day, Ed sees a giant hot air balloon flying over his house. He asks his Mum if they can go for a ride in a hot air balloon.

For his birthday, Ed's mum takes him for a ride in a hot air baloon. Ed is so excited!

Ed and his mum are about to go up in the hot air balloon. The balloon is filled with hot air, which makes it float.

Did You Know ?

A piball is used to steer the balloon.
It tells the pilot which way the wind is blowing.

The hot air comes from gas **burners**.

Bungee Jumping

Look at this! Bungee jumping is when you jump from somewhere high while you are **connected** to a cord.

Bungee jumpers wear a leg harness.
The harness is connected to a thick cord,
called the bungee cord.

Bungee jumpers leap off a high **platform**. When they jump, the bungee cord stretches.

The bungee jumper hangs upside down.
They swing on the bungee cord by their ankles.

People often bungee jump over rivers. Sometimes their hands even touch the water! After the jump, they are helped into a boat.

Ed loves watching extreme air sports. He can't wait to try some when he is older, too!

Glossary

base jumping jumping off solid objects, such as towers, bridges and cliffs

burners devices used to inflate hot air balloons

connected joined to

extreme going beyond the usual limits

harness a set of straps used to attach something

motor an engine, the thing that makes something go

platform a raised floor or surface

tandem one behind the other